Jamal Khan was born in London in 1961 as the son of a Pakistani father and a German mother.

When he was 2, his parents divorced and

Jamal and his older brother grew up in rather modest circumstances near Frankfurt, Germany, where they lived with their mother.

After earning a secondary school certificate in 10th grade, Jamal pursued vocational training at an exclusive wine store where he worked as a wine steward. Later, he joined the editorial department of an advertising-distribution company.

Dissatisfied with his job prospects, Jamal went back to school and earned the equivalent of his G.E.D. and then a degree in marketing/communications. From an entry-level job as a copy writer, he launched a career in advertising that led to positions as president of three different international companies and co-founder of another one, which was ultimately sold to an international agency.

After 25 years in the advertising industry, Jamal switched careers and co-founded a company that specializes in live streaming.

He lives near Frankfurt with his wife, son and a dog. The Billiard Strategy is his first book.

www.tredition.de

© 2013 Jamal Khan

Cover photo: © Sashkinw | Dreamstime.com

Publishing house: tredition GmbH, Hamburg

ISBN: 978-3-8491-8364-6

Printed in Germany

Jamal Khan

The Billiard Strategy

Your key to personal success!

"Paths are made by walking"

(Franz Kafka)

Preface

Plenty has been written about the subject "success"—reference materials range from scientific studies to conventional wisdom to esoteric literature.

The Billiard Strategy is based on a gleaning of facts and ideas from all of them, rather than a combination of them all. Fundamentally, it is an experience repeatedly tested over decades and proved successful.

I can attest to this so strongly because I am the one who has tested the effectiveness of the Billiard Strategy during my own career. When I was just starting out, I acted rather intuitively by setting out on a course of action without defining it in clear terms. Over the years, I gained additional insights from reading materials, lectures, presentations and experiences in daily life, which affirmed and reinforced what was initially more or less a gut feeling. Eventually, I solidified my own tactic and called it the Billiard Strategy.

The Billiard Strategy might become your personal key to success, too. With the conditional "might" being the operative word here because you decide what you will accomplish. This doesn't mean that you can plop down on your couch now and your life will turn out the way you want it to be simply because of the power of your thoughts. Not at all.

The point of the Billiard Strategy is not the simple self-affirmation of goals. Rather, the Strategy will teach you to develop a specific pattern of thinking and planning. If you can internalize this pattern, you will become less likely to react, but rather to act and thus reach your goals more easily.

One thing I can assure you right now: The appeal of the Billiard Strategy lies in its ease and simplicity! That may also be its detriment because many people might not want to try it, thinking life is this great mystery that cannot be easily understood, let alone changed.

I know this: I've always benefited from what I can understand easily. But everybody to his own: I don't want to impose the Billiard Strategy on anybody or pursue some vain attempt to convert humanity.

Those who like life complicated may continue to live like that—except that in my opinion, that's not the easy way to lead a happy, satisfying and productive life. Please don't misunderstand "productive"; a successful life is not necessarily expressed by your bank balance.

If you feel comfortable with "ease and simplicity," then reading this book will reward you with ways of thinking that will lead to changes in your life and a more confident outlook.

Because one thing is certain: Everybody whom I have talked to over the years about the Billiard Strategy has benefited from it in one way or another, regardless of their particular situation or size of problems. So I stand by my promise: The Billiard Strategy works in all circumstances and without any side effects.

"Just Do It!" is a well-known advertising slogan from a major athletics sportswear and equipment company. And that's what I want to advise you to do, just do it! The Billiard Strategy is very simple to follow as I am about to explain. You can read all about it in one sitting and start the process of implementing it into your own life immediately.

Whether you reach your goal very quickly or rather gradually—I wish you best of luck. I'd love to hear from you how the Billiard Strategy has led to positive changes in your life; please contact me at jamal.khan@live.de or post on my Facebook page at https://www.facebook.com/DieBillardStrategie.

Chapter 1
After that, nothing is going to be the same anymore

I am firmly convinced that this book could change your life significantly. To understand why I can be so sure, you will want to know how this book came about.

I used to mention the Billiard Strategy only if the opportunity was right. For example, some time ago, my wife and I met with another couple, friends of ours, at a restaurant. At some point, one of them, the woman, shared with us how she felt tormented by her new boss and how she didn't like her job anymore. Her work, which she used to enjoy for many years and do with a great deal of dedication, had become a source of great frustration and endless daily battles.

Her story wasn't news to us; she had told us a very similar tale of woe almost a year earlier when the new boss came onboard and immediately proved to be a know-it-all, micromanaging control freak.

Now my wife and I asked our friend why in the meantime she hadn't tried to look for a job at another organization. After all, good employees were always needed and she would most likely find something else. Besides, we felt that under such circumstances, it would be preferable to change jobs rather than deal with the daily aggravation and even get literally sick from it all.

Our friend offered the usual reasons why she hadn't tried to change her situation—starting from her good salary to the four-day work week to the convenient office location.

As plausible as all that sounded, the longer we discussed her situation, the more it became evident that the real reason for her inaction was fear of change, combined with certain inertia.

To be fair, our friend viewed her situation realistically: She fully understood that neither her boss nor her overall circumstances were likely to change on their own accord. It was up to her to either tolerate the situation or seek an alternative.

How familiar all this sounded: I had lived through a very similar situation many years ago. At that time, I too felt bullied by my boss, hated my job and was miserable, and yet, I literally tried to "sit out" the status quo.

I stayed in that job for almost two years, but nothing happened, or rather, nothing happened that I was hoping for. At the end, it was up to me to make things happen. True, according to the old adage "Man is a creature of habit," my two-year-long inactivity meant I was in good company, but that didn't make me feel better, rather to the contrary: The whole aggravation led to a stomach ulcer!

Feeling harassed at my job and feeling ill—I suffered mentally and physically. I was mad at myself and finally decided to make some changes so I wouldn't ever be caught in such a pickle again.

Yet how could I be certain that a future boss wouldn't be equally difficult? That's why I started searching for something that would remove this fear of change, something that would stop me from wasting my time treading water and getting sick in the process.

From today's point of view I can say this: My attitude was spot-on because it has protected my very sensitive stomach to this very day.

But what I cannot say in retrospect is this: Which came first, the strategy and then the image or first the image and then the strategy? You need to know that I am a visual learner and remember images more easily than verbal information. (Tell me your name and I am bound to forget it right away, but I'll be able to remember your face for years to come.) That's why I needed an appropriate mental picture for my strategy.

However, in the end it is not important which came first—the image of "billiard" encapsulated my thought processes brilliantly. Not only because I am a passionate billiard player, but also because it represented the perfect metaphor to illustrate the consequences of doing-nothing versus taking-action.

This is how the Billiard Strategy came about, even though I didn't openly express it then. At that point, it served solely for my own purposes as a mental metaphor to prompt me to action.

Only many years later did I begin to describe the Billiard Strategy to a buddy or two as a means of giving advice.

Just as I did on this particular evening: When I explained the Billiard Strategy to our friend, she became so enthusiastic, she immediately decided to give it a try as a way to get out of her job misery. (Incidentally, as soon as she started taking action, she was offered another position with a different company and gave notice. Today, she is very content and engaged at her new place of employment!)

I realized something else during that evening: Even though I had been using the Billiard Strategy for a long time, not many of my friends and acquaintances knew about it. That lack of awareness was probably my fault because not only did I rarely mention my methodology, but because I tend to come across as a positive individual anyway, the type that looks at the glass being half full, never half empty. Nobody suspected that a deliberate effort guided my upbeat attitude.

Even my wife, who had known me for almost 30 years, had no clue—frankly, I had never told her about the Billiard Strategy. Why would I? She is as optimistic about life as I am, and there had never been a situation where I considered it necessary to share my insights.

On our way home, she told me admiringly that the Billiard Strategy had painted a very clear picture for our friend. Who had come up with this metaphor, she asked. When I told her, she initially thought I was joking. But then she suggested that the Billiard Strategy could probably help a great many people—and hence, the idea for this book was born.

No sooner said than done. So if you are curious now to learn how the Billiard Strategy works, I am curious to know what value it will add to your life. And I don't mean solely financially, but in general. After you've read this book, you'll understand what I mean. Because one important insight is this:

Once you've set something in motion, nothing is going to be the same anymore—that's why even the smallest "nudge" can be meaningful.

Chapter 2
Do you have a problem?

If you think that your situation is very different from my friend's, ask yourself this key question: Are you truly content with the way things are?

I purposely kept this question rather general so that you can answer it without much thought: "Sure, I am super, I am doing just fine. I have a great job or a great spouse or great kids or a great house or a great car," or whatever it is that is near and dear to your heart. You could also say, "I am in good health and in good spirits, why should anything bother me?"

But it's not for nothing that I asked this key question, which really aims at the core of any issue. I do know that introspection tends to make people uncomfortable because it forces them to face certain truths they'd rather avoid. Why? As soon as they have admitted to themselves that they are unhappy with certain things in life, they know they ought to change them; nobody likes to live in a long-term state of self-deception.

However, until most people reach the point where they decide to make certain changes—regardless of whether they initiate these changes themselves or the changes are forced upon them—the adage of "humans are creatures of habit" applies. Consequently, the subject of change is postponed, avoided and denied as long as possible.

Therefore: Is there something you know you ought to tackle and yet you keep procrastinating? Then the Billiard Strategy will teach you that changes can be positive—especially if you make the first move and are able to control these changes to some degree.

That doesn't mean that you'll be able to control everything in your life just as soon as you've finished reading this book. Certainly not! Life is full of detours and distractions and offers many surprises big and small. What you will discover, though, is this: You'll stop "treading water" and you'll notice new opportunities, new ways and possibilities that you'll be able to explore and pursue.

So, if there is a situation you've been meaning to change for some time now but didn't, stop making excuses, especially to yourself.

For example: If you don't enjoy your current job anymore, don't listen any longer to this little voice in your head that tells you stuff like "I am earning good money" or "It's job security" or "I have been so busy I simply haven't had time to look for something else."

Simply start making some changes. That doesn't mean you'll want to resign on the spot. Nor does it mean you'll magically find another job in the next day or two. But it does mean that you will take a first step. You might only need a few more, perhaps small steps, until you reach your goal. Be prepared to take a few steps sideways, maybe even backwards, before you push forward again.

This "step by step" approach is a typical element of the Billiard Strategy. It will teach you how to become very flexible in your course of action. You don't need detailed planning—you just start. One thing is certain:

As soon as you get up and start moving, no matter the direction, you'll notice how everything around you will also start changing.

Chapter 3
Get rid of negative thoughts

Before you'll learn all about the Billiard Strategy, you'll want to get into the right frame of mind: practice positive thinking! I know that this is not necessarily easy and not always possible. If you are the type of person who thinks both positively and negatively or more negatively than positively, you should find this subject especially important.

Now, in order to be a positive thinker, you don't have to view the world through the proverbial rose-colored glasses or act like a Pollyanna. Remember this basic axiom: Whether you are hoping for something good or expecting something bad to happen, you can't predict the outcome.

You can only assume that one or the other will happen.

Hence, think about your situation rationally. Visualize how things might pan out—best and worst case scenario—and what either outcome will mean for you personally. But don't worry about anything at this point.

Simply thinking about the future is neither good nor bad, it is neutral. You can't predict what will happen, but you can influence what will happen.

That's because your attitude plays a significant role in all circumstances. You're familiar with the term "self-fulfilling prophecy"? It means that any expectations, positive or negative, about a particular event cause people to behave in ways that fulfill the expectations. The logical opposite is "self-destroying prophesy," which occurs when people engage in behaviors to prevent a prediction or generalization.

Both terms were coined by the American sociologist Robert K. Meron on the basis of the Thomas theorem, which states that perception creates its own reality. Put differently, the interpretation of a situation causes the action. The concept refers to the wide gap between subjective and objective reality.

This may sound a bit too abstract, so let me give you a simple example: As I am writing this book, I cannot control its future success or failure. Whether somebody will read it one day is something I have absolutely no control over. So there is no point in fretting over it.

I'd rather imagine that my book is going to be a huge hit! It's tempting to revel in positive reviews (imaginary at this point), but I am also willing to consider its possible failure. At the very least, I will have tried publishing my book, and if it will have helped even only a single reader, my efforts will have been worthwhile.

Do you notice something? I accomplished several goals with my musings about the future, which as I want to point out again, I am unable to change: First, I bolstered my self-confidence and feel energized to continue writing no matter how exhausting it is. Second, visualizing how my book is going to be a winner helps me write a good book. Third, I am prepared to find a silver lining in the event that my work won't enjoy widespread popularity but will only be read by my immediate family and friends.

In other words, instead of saddling myself with negative thoughts about my published book, I have encouraged myself. Now I am actually looking forward to everything connected with this project.

Please don't think I have made it too easy for myself because this is precisely the point: If you face an important challenge, analyze it rationally. Don't be guided by emotions or by the opinions of others, and you'll discover that negative messages are counterproductive.

Makes sense, right? If you anticipate a negative outcome from the get-go—even though you haven't a faintest clue how everything will turn out—you're just setting yourself up for failure!

You'll start your task with a negative outlook even before anything unpleasant happens. Your lack of motivation makes it harder for you to get going and, if you're part of a team, saps everybody else's energy and goodwill, both at home and at work.

If you tend to take life too seriously, don't blame your circumstances. Let's be honest: Your attitude is at fault.

People who tend to think negatively always find things to criticize. Even if things are perfect, they don't believe in their own success until, not surprisingly, it eludes them. What these negative thinkers don't realize is that they are living out a "self-fulfilling prophesy"; they anticipate something bad, therefore, it happens.

Should you look at life through rose-colored glasses? As I said before, of course not. But you should understand the harmful effects of negative thinking.

Anticipating the worst won't shield you from disappointments, but it will rob you of the energy and hope that you need to improve your situation. Instead of worrying needlessly and doing nothing to avoid set-backs, look at challenges and opportunities realistically. Yes, even plan for failure, but don't let that tear you down. Rather, try to come up with a reasonable assessment of your chances of success.

Take your cue from sports: Every athlete or player knows that every game, every round, every match can be won—or lost. That is true for football, golf or Monopoly. They play anyway. That's how it is in life: Win some, lose some. Which is how you've just learned another component of the Billiard Strategy?

Only those who take action minimize their risk; worrying and doing nothing is more likely to result in failure.

Chapter 4
Useless emotions are out of place

You probably already know intuitively that negative thoughts are counterproductive. And still, it might be difficult to always approach challenges with a positive outlook.

Look at it this way: Not all situations require you to become emotionally engaged, and certainly not those that are likely to elicit a negative reaction.

Consider furthermore: If you allow yourself to give in to negative emotions, you set yourself up to notice nothing but dangers and possible pitfalls, concentrate on people's weaknesses rather than strengths, and focus on every single flaw of this world.

I tend to become very emotional and know how difficult it can be to stay rational. I don't mean to imply that I am naïve and gullible. Nor am I saying that I refuse to give in to my emotions and refrain from laughing, crying or screaming. However, if I look at the issues at hand purely rationally, I am much less fearful of failure.

In addition, I am more likely to solve any setbacks without being overwhelmed by negative emotions.

Thus, if you do likewise, that is, choose to think rationally, you'll inevitably focus on the successful outcome of your mission. That attitude, in turn, will enable you to find intuitively the right approach to bring your project to a successful conclusion.

So, instead of getting yourself all worked up about what could go wrong, think positively. Evaluate all possible scenarios—good and bad—but make sure you stay rational. Don't be naïve and consider only the good because sometimes things do go wrong. Instead, take into account all possible outcomes and you'll automatically decide to pursue a positive course of action. And if things do fail or turn out differently than planned—well, you won't be crushed by disappointment because you had already allowed for that possibility.

This is all theory for now. In practical terms, you are the one who will decide what you want to do and how. What does that mean? You'll decide the best solution to your current problem and determine how to achieve that goal by developing methods for enhancement, researching new ideas and possibilities and visualizing various changes. In short, you are busy mapping out a goal-oriented strategy. The nice side effect? All of a sudden, you find yourself highly motivated.

The more options you consider, the more assured you'll feel about your chances of success. So focus on your goals and how you are going to get there, and you'll slowly abandon all negative thinking.

This is another important element of the Billiard Strategy:

Get your thoughts under control, avoid negative emotions and set your own course of action.

Chapter 5
Small cause, big effect

In 1963, by sheer happenstance, the U.S. meteorologist Edward Lorenz made an important discovery: When using a numerical computer model to rerun a weather prediction, he inadvertently input only three places after the decimal point, instead of the usual six. To his great surprise, the result was much different than expected, and he was dumbfounded. How could that be, given the minute change to the original calculation?

After he ruled out any computer malfunctions, he concluded what might sound banal at first: Small causes can have big effects.

Lorenz continued to study this phenomenon, which has since become known around the world as the "butterfly effect." His theory: Does the flap of a butterfly's wings in Brazil set off a tornado in Texas? His conclusion: Weather has to be studied globally, which is why it cannot be forecast long-term. The interactions are simply too complex. Even an infinitesimal change in the starting conditions of a system will result in dramatically different outputs for that system. Hence: Weather is fundamentally chaotic.

According to the ensuing chaos theory, not just weather is unpredictable. There are situations in everyday life that cannot be calculated mathematically, for example, a dripping faucet. To this very day, nobody can predict after how many seconds it will "plop" again.

Ditto for traffic jams: it's impossible to say in advance when and why they will occur and for how long. We can all share personal experiences about "chaotic traffic."

Some predictions and calculations are possible even with chaotic systems. These are considered deterministic, which means their behavior can be determined with certain equations. Yet the type of chaos defined by Lorenz and many other researchers eludes all scientific explanations. One such system is the game of billiards, or pool, as it is commonly known in the United States.

Imagine the ideal game of pool: The cue ball is supposed to roll across the table in a perfect line to collide with one or several balls. The player aims to plan the direction and impact of his shot precisely. But can even a world champion with perfect control predict exactly how the ball's path will pan out? The tiniest unpredicted spin would cause the ball to deflect from its intended course after just an inch or two and hence, render any prediction null and void. This deflection would increase exponentially as the round cue ball moves on and collides with yet more balls. The results are obvious: Even the tiniest miscalculation of the cue ball's projected path would magnify the original error with each subsequent collision. In other words: The initial cause, an insignificant miscalculation per se, has an impact of extraordinary consequences.

From that point of view, the game of billiards is absolute chaos. So why should you trust the Billiard Strategy? Very simple:

By following the Billiard Strategy, you won't change your future—it is simply too complex. But you will improve your starting position!

Chapter 6
The Billiard Strategy

You now know the basic principle of the Billiard Strategy. But maybe you've never played the actual game before? So before elaborating on the Strategy, I'll briefly explain the game itself. Let's look at pool or pocket-billiards, which is the American-style variation, arguable the easiest to play and readily explainable.

Put simply, when playing pool, two players use tapered sticks called cues to strike a cue ball, usually white, in order to shoot a total of 15 balls (seven striped balls, seven solid-colored balls and one black 8 ball) into six pockets (one in each corner, two along the side rails). Only the cue ball may come into contact with the cues.

To start the game, the balls are placed into a triangular rack. The player chosen to shoot first attempts to break the rack apart. Depending on the type of the first ball pocketed, solid or stripes, the player continues to try to pocket balls of only that type, "his" type.

If he doesn't manage to pocket, it's the other player's turn. Players may only pocket the black 8 ball once the other balls have been pocketed. The player who sinks the black ball wins.

Billiards has numerous variations, which to explain here would go too far. In other words, so much for the game itself—let's apply these lessons to real life to meet the Billiard Strategy!

For right now, let's forget the second player; we'll talk about him later. Crucial is the cue ball because it represents your level of activity. Whatever your current challenge or problem may be—as you are pondering what to do about it and how to proceed— imagine yourself in the position of the cue ball as the game is about to start.

The ball is facing 15 balls, arranged in a triangular rack because that's how the game begins. As long as those balls are simply positioned within the rack, nothing is going to change: a cue ball is lying on a pool table facing 15 balls arranged in a triangular rack.

So there you have your playing field. You are allowed to move your cue ball as long as it stays within the boundaries of the rails.

Let's apply that principle to your real-life playing field. You have to play by the rules of the game (as set by your family, community, friends, employer, co-workers, as well as official laws and regulations), but you have some flexibility about what you are going to do next and how.

You could do nothing, but that would be foolish. And yet—that's precisely what many do. Instead of actively trying to change their current situation, many remain inactive. They tread water and wait to see what will happen.

Consider that inertia from the point of view of the cue ball: If it remained in place, would anything change? Absolutely nothing. The cue ball wouldn't advance a single fraction of an inch and your perspective of the game would stay stagnant.

In contrast, imagine what would happen if you strike the cue ball with the tip of your cue? It would start moving, even if you don't strike it particularly hard. The point is, the cue ball is moving. Otherwise, it would be your opponent's turn and you might lose the entire game.

Let's assume you set the cue ball on its way, but your aim is tentative and the ball doesn't have much oomph. It heads toward the rack but is likely to come to a full stop before breaking the balls apart.

According to pool rules, now it's your opponent's turn. According to the Billiard Strategy, it's still your turn because what counts is that you got your cue ball moving, that is, you got yourself moving! Your world already looks very different. The triangular rack, which just a short while ago was located quite a ways away, is now close in front of you. So close you can—metaphorically speaking—clearly see each individual ball.

Let's apply that to real life and imagine that each ball represents an opportunity or possibility for change. You could say that you have moved much closer to each opportunity and have a much better view point how each might pan out. You notice details you couldn't observe before simply because they were too far away.

Even if you don't care to view these details close up—at least you've taken the first step. You are on your way and you will find out that taking the second step might not be a big deal.

In other words: Even if your original goal seemed forever beyond your reach, by taking one step at a time—no matter how small—you'll get there. If, by contrast, you never take a shot at that cue ball—you in this metaphor—in the first place, your goal will stay a dream never to be realized.

Now, don't stop there. Don't relax and think, "That was easy." It's not enough to take just that single first step. As long as it's the other player's turn and you stand idly by, you are likely to lose the game.

Let me interject here: Losing per se is not a bad thing. Even champions can't win every single time! If they lose, of course they are upset, that's human nature. But do you think for a moment they quit for good just as soon as they lose a single game? Of course not.

They get over it. They learn from their losses and consider another experience and situation that will help them get better in their game. That's how each defeat can help them improve and become more successful players. It's that old adage: Practice makes perfect.

However, in real life a lot of folks make the mistake of allowing the first setback to get them off course. They might have started a new venture full of enthusiasm and dedication, but if the envisioned success doesn't materialize overnight, they quit.

They don't ever try again because "things just weren't working out." Don't be like them. Instead, think like a world champion. You can't win every single match, but you can learn from every single one of them and improve your game.

Don't be discouraged if you start on a course of action and things then turn out very differently. Don't forget that both a simple game of pool and your complex future are governed by chaos and can be altered by the most minute incidents. Like the weather, both are entirely unpredictable no matter what you dream of or what others tell you will happen.

Picture yourself playing pool and taking aim to break the rack apart. Within seconds, the playing field will look very different, especially if you go for a powerful shot and manage a full hit.

The balls scatter in all directions, strike the rails and roll all over the table. Maybe this ball or that is sunk, some balls collide and disperse, one ball just wants to keep on rolling, and so forth. The most important observation is this: the cue ball ends up in a location very different from where a weak breaking shot would have placed it. Now you are no longer simply noticing details, you're noticing chances.

Now that you are past the initial goal of just getting the ball going, you are faced with a whole set of new opportunities. Maybe you manage to pocket a ball or two or even win?

In any case, you have the chance to do just that. Of course, just because the playing field may look very attractive at this point doesn't guarantee your win. What counts is this, just as in real life: If you keep moving, you will find new ways and opportunities. If you stay put, nothing will change.

Or rather, everything around you keeps changing. Whether you have one opponent or several team players—they all have goals they want to reach and in going after them, they change your "playing field."

So here is the deal: If you play it safe and attempt nothing, your surroundings will force changes on you anyway. Those changes may happen from one second to the next or take days, weeks, months or even years—depending on how irritating, threatening or destructive you perceive those changes to be.

Changes will catch up with you eventually, and it is latest at this point that you've will have begun moving. Unfortunately, you'll probably have fewer options now. To make matters worse, you may find yourself pressed for time or lack the energy and frame of mind to explore new ventures. You may have to take the next best thing.

That may be a good thing—if you're lucky. Otherwise, tough luck. Therefore, you should heed this:

If you always wait for things to happen, you don't have the option to act, but are forced to react. And if you react, you're likely to find yourself with fewer options or in a losing position.

Chapter 7
Think positive

Now you know what the Billiard Strategy is all about. As I said earlier, it is relatively simple to understand. The key is to keep moving; like the cue ball, you want to stay in motion.

As long as you move along, everything around you changes: Nothing remains as it once was. The more you move, the less likely you will end up in your exact starting position. And as you discover more opportunities and possibilities, you'll also find more ways to take advantages of your options.

For this strategy to work best, you will want to look at the world and your life in a positive light. If you perceive life as a constant battle, it will remain a constant battle. With that attitude, you are probably going to approach the Billiard Strategy with a loser mentality and accept whatever fate befalls you.

Please review the earlier chapter of this book again to lay that excuse to rest once and for all: It is simply not true that things happen or don't happen simply because of fate. Instead, your outlook on life greatly influences the course of events.

In this sense, look at life like a game, rather than a battle: Of course you might lose an individual round or match, but you won't suffer a final defeat. Remember that you always have the option of challenging your opponent to another match! New game, new luck, right?

So don't try to pursue your goals with a do-or-die attitude. You are just making matters worse. Don't overthink and overwork your strategies either; just get going—everything else will fall into its place.

The nice thing about the Billiard Strategy: You yourself determine your speed, your direction and your methods.

So don't waste energy second-guessing your choices, just move your cue ball. It's entirely up to you how you place your shots and what avenues open up for you.

Not convinced? If you don't believe that the mere thought of a game of pool will "result" in anything, consider this: Thoughts are not "little nothings." Instead, and you may already know this, they are a series of signals that trigger electrical and chemical reactions in your brain. Even if you don't feel them as those processes happen automatically, your thoughts are actual forces.

A single external stimulus or signal prompts numerous transactions in your brain as it releases chemical neurotransmitters that cause the central nervous system to respond and react.

As we are "thinking," we are not aware of all the hard work our brain is doing. Nor can we immediately process with full understanding all those pieces of information that our subconscious mind stores.

Let's look at the subconscious mind. Psychologists use this term to refer to that part of our human psyche that is not immediately accessible to our conscious mind. Furthermore, most of our behavior is directed by our subconscious mind.

In the 1980s, the American neurologist Benjamin Libet made headlines with the results of his "Libet experiments." He measured how much time passes before a subject performs a consciously chosen action.

Taking Libet's observations a step further, the German biologist and neurologist Gerhard Roth discovered that what the mind perceives to be consciously chosen actions are really the result of complex subconscious processes.

In other words, while we may still be mulling over an issue, our subconscious mind has already made a decision. Neurological studies have shown that our subconscious mind moves faster than the conscious mind.

That allows an interesting conclusion: After our subconscious mind has reached a decision, our conscious mind gets busy coming up with a logical explanation for it—after the fact. Perhaps to give us inner peace.

Of course, many other explanations and observations about the subconscious mind do exist—but none question its fundamental influence over our psyche and behavior. That leads to a different question: What is stored in our subconscious mind and how does it direct our actions?

Since we were born, our subconscious mind has stored patterns of words, thoughts and much more. Some of this gets very firmly anchored, regardless of whether we initiated the actions or others and regardless of whether the experiences were relevant, useful or valuable.

Over time, through this type of self-programming, if you will, our subconscious mind has built a data base of often-repeated notions and behaviors. As we are creatures of habit, our brain tends to reuse past behavior patterns again and again.

Unfortunately, those are not necessarily healthy thought patterns. Especially unpleasant or self-limiting "programs" tend to re-appear often and send warning signals about dire consequences as soon as we entertain certain ideas.

The brain doesn't care whether thoughts and behaviors from your self-programmed data base are good or bad. Like a computer, it simply processes whatever action it stored on its "hard drive." In short, our subconscious directs our voluntary actions.

But that's not all: Hardly anybody manages to block out all self-doubts. And that sets you off on a path of more destructive self-programming, so you're caught in a vicious cycle.

For example, how do you think you will succeed at something if you talk yourself out of it from the start? You know the excuses: "I am not going to accomplish anything," or "I got off to a bad start," or "I won't manage," or "I haven't got the time," or "I won't have any luck."

You get the idea. You can probably list additional excuses and know how to apply them to any situation and challenge. This type of mental self-programming rules our life; we started doing that as little kids and add more as we grow older.

Put it all together and you're looking at your own unique qualifications to "play." They may work for or against you, help you along or set you back, propel you forward in leaps and bounds or stop you dead in your tracks.

So never underestimate the workings and the power of your mind. Looking at it positively, you're in charge of what you want to "program" next!

Why? Your subconscious doesn't care where the next impressions come from or how. It accepts everything you feed it, whether it's a fleeting thought or a conversation with yourself, whether you're right on target or off-base, whether the new stuff makes you happy or miserable. That's why you want to stick to this guideline: Think positively, and positive results will come.

You can't change your future entirely, but you can make your dreams come true—to some extent! That's because you can control your attitude, and your way of thinking can influence how you'll play your game and how far you want to go.

After all, aside from your genetic makeup and any traits you have inherited from your ancestors, you are the one who sets your cue ball rolling.

Whatever negative thought and behavior patterns you may have acquired in the past, you are able to change those anytime. Maybe on your own, maybe with the help of a therapist.

If you are not taking charge of this "reprogramming" of your subconscious, you'll remain dependent on the "indoctrination" by your surroundings: your parents, your teachers, your past experiences, your general environment—in short, the hang-ups and whims of people around you.

For the same reason, it's also useless, for example, for you to point fingers and assign blame to somebody else for your past failures and setbacks.

Don't fool yourself: Your present is as it is and the past was as it was—you can't change either. What you can do is this: Influence your future. From now on, "play" every second the way you want your life to turn out.

And so, in the spirit of the Billiard Strategy, keep nudging yourself forward. Because one thing is certain:

How you direct your thoughts is up to you— you control at all times how to play "your game."

Chapter 8
Start playing

Even the greatest athletes don't achieve their peak performance at every single event.

If that happens, it's usually because they literally talk themselves out of success. They succumb to negative internal messages. For example, instead of encouraging themselves with the words, "I'll come in first," they tell themselves, "I will not come in last." Their mind translates that to mean, "I won't win."

A German scientist and coach, Hans Eberspächer, who researched mental training during his academic and professional career, once put it this way: "Through self-talk, we establish a strategy for our actions, give ourselves directions, organize our thoughts and examine our activities."

Without realizing it, most of us tend to have a running dialogue with ourselves throughout the day, and as these random and purposeful thoughts cross our minds, faulty thinking and negative notions will occur. But in order to be successful—in any walk of life—it is vital to get a handle on our self talk, that little voice in our head.

In sports psychology, it is now common to teach the ability to develop positive self talk. Elite athletes undergo regular training to replace negative self talk with more positive messages. Over time and with repetition, champions develop a new habit of thinking positive statements and messages, which in turn bolsters their physical performance. Trust me, you don't need to be a top athlete to use this technique to improve your chances of success.

To motivate yourself successfully, you need self-esteem. Self-esteem, in turn, largely depends on how you see yourself: If you believe in your abilities and skills, you will be able to put them to good use. If, in contrast, you are your own worst critic, your self-esteem will be quite low. In that case, forget self-motivation.

There is an obvious solution: Don't focus on your weaknesses, but on your strengths! If you do that, you'll be able to "reprogram" your thought patterns: Visualize yourself having reached your goal after mastering all challenges along the way.

Be sure not to put things negatively, such as "I am not unhappy," which your mind tends to subvert into "I am unhappy." Simply say, "I am happy."

Here is another tip: Don't give yourself long, drawn-out instructions that get you all muddled. Stick to simple directives. Think these directives, hum them, sing them to yourself or whatever you want to do; it doesn't really matter. You can also write them out on index cards that you review throughout your day. Or paper your walls and mirrors at home with Post-it notes.

Typically, it takes about 40 days until you've "re-programmed" your mind. With some folks, it takes a bit longer, with others a bit less. No matter how long, you'll eventually start noticing the results of your efforts. You begin feeling more hopeful and more confident, and you'll probably start accomplishing some of your goals. The key is to create positive instructions to create new thinking patterns in your subconscious. A mere "I can manage" or "I can do this" can create miracles. The advantage of these positive affirmations is not that you start looking at everything in the best possible light—very unlikely— but that you become focused again on your strengths. When that happens, you are more aware of how you think—positively, of course—regardless of whether good or bad things happen to you.

That brings me to the end of my discussion of the Billiard Strategy. I hope you'll agree that I didn't promise you something I didn't deliver. You have learned that even a tiny nudge will move your cue ball across your personal playing field, i.e., set a plan of action in motion. That's infinitely preferable to doing nothing else but sitting back and waiting. Have no fear that this nudge will "harm" you in any way. Rather, it will open up new opportunities and prospects for you. Don't allow negative feelings or debilitating self-doubts to control your life. Make up your mind to "reprogram" your subconscious the way top athletes train their mental state of mind and encourage yourself each day to stay focused on your goals. In other words: Don't sit around and allow others to dictate your next steps and decisions. Don't act as if you are dependent on the orders of others.

You have the determination, the know-how, and now, the Billiard Strategy to take charge of our life—do it, you only live once!

As a final word, I want to leave you with a quote from Friedrich Schiller, one of Germany's finest poets and philosophers, which says it all: **Man only plays when in the full meaning of the word he is a man, and he is only completely a man when he plays.**

Don't forget

Once you've set something in motion, nothing is going to be the same anymore—that's why even the smallest "nudge" can be meaningful.

As soon as you get up and start moving, no matter the direction, you'll notice how everything around you will also start changing.

Only those who take action minimize their risk; worrying and doing nothing is more likely to result in failure.

Get your thoughts under control, avoid negative emotions and set your own course of action.

By following the Billiard Strategy, you won't change your future—it is simply too complex. But you will improve your starting position!

If you always wait for things to happen, you don't have the option to act, but are forced to react. And if you react, you're likely to find yourself with fewer options or in a losing position.

How you direct your thoughts is up to you—you control at all times how to play "your game."

About tredition

tredition is a publishing house based in Hamburg, Germany.

Incorporated in 2006 by Sandra Latusseck and Soenke Schulz, tredition started out as a self-publishing service provider for book publications in Germany.

In this sector tredition set the goal for itself to provide the best and fairest publishing service to authors and other publishing houses. In order to do so, tredition developed several tools for automated publication of books in e-Book and printed format.

These tools are now used in the process to publish 100,000 titles in the world's largest book series TREDITION CLASSICS.

Zeitfracht Medien GmbH
Ferdinand-Jühlke-Straße 7
99095 Erfurt, Deutschland
produktsicherheit@kolibri360.de